Do You See Them?
In the Garden

Sandra Williamson
The Spirit Realm Series

Do You See Them?
In the Garden
ISBN 9780997612431

Copyright © 2015 by Sandra Willamson

Published by Winters Publishing Group

Book development and editing services by Winters Publishing Group.

Printed in the United States of America. All rights reserved under United States and International Copyright Law. Contents and/or cover may not be reproduced in whole or in part in any form without the express written consent of the author or publisher.

Dedication

To my precious grandchildren, Gabriel and Justice, who are gifted to see both naturally and spiritually. May the Lord increase your vision to see all things clearly and to live powerfully in all of His creation!

Before anything was made,

Before even one thing was created

There was nothing

...but God!

He has always been, everywhere!
He is not in outer space ....

He IS all space!
He IS all Light!

God is everywhere and everything about Him is good!

God is made up of three persons:

The Father,

the Son,

and the Holy Spirit.

They are like a family.
They all think the same, but they have different jobs.

God created everything!
He made Heaven and all the things in Heaven.
He made the Angels and gave them all jobs too!
Angels always love doing their jobs!

God made a very special Garden on the Earth. He made sunshine, water, plants and trees for food, He made animals too!

And then God made a woman! God loved the people He made!

But God told Lucifer he could not stay in Heaven because he would not follow God's rules.

(Not following God's rules is called "sin," and sin is doing something against God.)

Satan made a plan to trick Adam and Eve.
He wanted them to do what God had told them not to do.

Satan lied to Adam and Eve. He told them it was ok to eat the fruit from the tree God had told them not to eat.

Now God was so sad.
He told them they could not stay in the Garden.
Just like Heaven, the Garden belonged to God.
Only good things can stay in God's good places.

But God had a great plan!
God the Son, Jesus, was on His way to help Adam and Eve!
He would show Adam and Eve
how to escape from Satan and find their way back to God!

Coming Soon in the "Do You See Them?" series:

Book#2- "Do You See Them"
Discovering God's Ways

The classic stories tell of all manner of miracles. What if you could see behind the scenes the roles the angels played? Daniel surely wasn't alone in the lion's den; Shadrach, Mesheck and Abendigo absolutely had unseen help in the fiery furnace; and Jonah in the whale was clearly preserved at the Lord's instruction. Read and discover!

Book#3- "Do You See Them?"
I See Jesus!

This book reveals Jesus and His amazing miracles, the people that He touched, and how Satan tried to stop Him. Father God sent His Son to demonstrate Heaven coming to earth. A spiritual upheaval takes place as the world submits to the Lord's commands! Look and see!

Book#4- "Do You See Them?"
God Wants to Use Me!

The fourth book in this series shows how God used ordinary people to do extraordinary things! Follow Peter and Paul as they speak healing to the lame man, preach the Good News, and teach the new church how to follow Jesus! Courage and strength in the Lord are learned in these New Testament stories that reveal just how many of God's helpers are surrounding us all the time. Say "Yes" and go!

Book#5- "Do You See Them?"
The King's Return

One day soon, Jesus will return to the earth. He is coming for His people, and He is zealous to bring His people, His Bride, to His Kingdom! Jesus comes to rescue His people from the hands of the enemy, once and for all! A whirlwind of the power and might of God are seen as the last attempts of the enemy to stop God's people from following Him are finally thwarted! Look up!

We hope you enjoyed the first book in the "Do You See Them?" series. Yet it doesn't end here. As Adam and Eve leave the special Garden, God already had a rescue plan in place. His goodness and kindness is all around them as He begins to teach mankind His ways. The "Do You See Them?" series is a peek into what is already happening all around us, everyday, unseen.

Watch for the next books in the "Do You See Them" series coming soon!

To order copies of the "Do You See Them?" book series, go to:
www.DoYouSeeThem.com or www.SpiritRealmSeries.com

About the Author

Sandra Williamson has a heart for children and delights in teaching them natural and spiritual realities. One of Sandra's greatest joys is to teach children the reality of the Word of God in pictures and stories.

Sandra grew up struggling with issues that could now be attributed to Autism Spectrum Disorders. She was diagnosed with 'brain astigmatism' as an adolescent and was not able to even accomplish high school. While raising her children, Sandra became desperate to find a way to extricate herself from the grasp of the disorder. Through continual prayer and rigorous study, Sandra was able to finish high school at age 28 and went on to pursue higher education. Sandra now holds a bachelor's certification in paralegal studies from California State University, a bachelor's degree in psychology from Oklahoma State University, and master's degree in human relations from the University of Oklahoma.

Sandra is the Founder and Executive Director of an international spiritual freedom and emotional healing ministry, "God's E.R." (*Emergency Restoration*), helping hundreds of individuals each year find the Truth of the Word of God to become healed in the whole person. Sandra's career has been an ongoing combination of ministry and natural support, always with the goal of helping others at the heart of her efforts.

Sandra Williamson is an ordained minister who lives in Tulsa, Oklahoma with her husband, James Williamson. The Williamson's are blessed to have four adult children and five grandchildren. Sandra is the author of the *Do Your See Them?* children series, and *Say,'Yes!'* (2014), a vision of the Bride of Christ.

www.ingramcontent.com/pod-product-compliance
Lightning Source LLC
LaVergne TN
LVHW070949070426
835507LV00030B/3470